One Lone Minstrel

One Lone Minstrel

by
Marv Ward

Broad River Books
Chapin, SC

Broad River Books
is an imprint of
MuddyFordPress.com

Library of Congress Number:2017907527

ISBN: 978-1-942081-11-1

Table of Contents

Introduction

I first met the Reverend Marv Ward in Rosewood at the old Utopia Bar. He had just finished a set and had been drinking a bit. He sat next to me at the bar and we talked. We talked of gigs, drinking, and women. This was his life, his music, and his addiction.

Marv is not your typical poet and this is not your typical book of poetry; this is a blues lyricist putting meat on the bones of songs as he sits at a bar and tells you what was and what could have been.

I invite you to read, 'One Lone Minstrel' and follow the Reverend Marv Ward as he leaves his blues upon the pages of his first book of poetic verse and imagine him in a side street bar standing at a mic, guitar slung over his shoulder, a half finished drink sits on an amp, and he sings,

> *"The blood of passion*
> *rises and flows*
> *and I have no*
> *tourniquet"*

Let him sing you more poems of love remembered and love lost and later, when his voice is hoarse or the booze runs out, sit at the bar with Marv and ask him to recite all that he has written of a bluesman's life lived in shades of indigo.

Al Black

ONE LONE MINSTREL

So sad to

see one lone minstrel

playing for the ghosts

of butterflies

who have flown with the cold.

Only shadows

dance now

in those glades of elven revelry,

and the trees do not speak

for there is no one

to listen.

WILD FLOWERS

I should go walking
    for wild flowers today,
        fill my vases.
The air in my room
    is so stale,
but I'll sit here
    and play my songs
to that portrait
    neatly framed
        in my heart
and dream
    of times when wildflowers
        grew in my backyard.

WASTELAND

Barren are the landscapes before me.

I walk through endless caverns

    etching epitaphs

        to forgotten souls.

Hard rock

    glistens

        in white hot heat.

Desert lizards scamper through

    my dazed trances.

        Singing single syllables

send me racing down the cliffs

    of new tomorrows

and echo

    resounding images of

        lost lingerings.

SWAMPED

I sit here,

swamped

    legs thrash

        but no hold,

sucking for breath

    slowly, slowly

        going under.

if I could just reach that branch

    the leaves flick so slowly in the wind

        as if time did no exist.

But time,

    like the breeze

    passes,

always there but always moving.

    My move,

        no time,

Cyclone wind and time

    blow back on each other

    and all things race

    by

        too fast

and time is so slow

    as I sit here

        swamped,

            waiting to go under.

SPRING

Bacchus sows green lust through the great heartland

    as all living creatures sing his name

       and beckon the sun.

Splashing through gossamer green lilies,

    his daughters

       giggle

          and smile

             the smile of innocence betrayed.

Their bodies

    symphonies of sensuous sight

       simmer in the sanguine sun

          searing the touch

             so it may never stray

    sighing

       they sing their siren songs.

Small birds echo the melodies

    from tall yellow pines

       to the great gleaming moon

          bathed in mountain mist

and the ghosts of ancient wanderers

    tell timeless tales of truth

       never-ending.

10:45 AND HOLDING

You know you will receive no call this night
no words of love
will be spoken to you.
You sit in silent solitude
studying the seams of your existence,
her voice
the only fruit that can satiate
your hunger.
You know there will be no call.
Still you wait,
is it madness,
are you a fool,
or just
too tired to do anything else?
Laying your head back upon the chair,
you raise your eyes to the ceiling
and paint your life
as you would see it,
colorful,
but neatly lavish
with no gray frayed edges.
If the phone would just ring,
you could be there
aloft in your dreams
and in those fleeting moments

while her voice

    intercourses with

        your mind and soul

            through aural orifice,

                your dreams would come true.

You know she will not call.

She is busy.

    Her world dances about her.

        Unknown frolickers

            pulling her life strings

                marionette arabesque

                through the air

    crashing into feelings,

        dangling

            from pleasure to despair.

Catching her in the dark,

    you give her your heart's razor edge

        to cut her strings

        to float free

            free with love

                free to will her

                    free to float

                      away.

You know she will not call.

MY CHESHIRE CAT

As I walk along the path

    I see you

        perched benignly on a limb above,

smiling

      and waging your tail.

I am awed

    as you pull truth from the shadows,

       illuminate the way.

But every time I come near

    you disappear

      only to reappear,

        laughing from the other side.

Then,

    just when

      at long last,

you let me come close enough to scratch behind an ear,

    you are gone

      with only a smile left

        to follow into oblivion.

BAR NAPKIN BLUES

Time flows

    and goes by,

        passing the waiting onlookers.

Currents, turbulent and unrelenting, waft over us.

We clutch at floating debris

    and struggle against the tide,

        but the river of time is flooding

            out of control

                and we drown in the depths of it.

And suddenly amidst the confusion

    clarity

        the light at the end of the tunnel vision.

        The struggles of life

    fall away into the abyss of unconscious bliss.

You order another drink

    care not for the consequence.

The passing parade

    rises and moves,

        filling the streets with passion,

            and I let myself be swept away,

            never wondering where

                I will be.

I will be wherever.

The fates play

and pull our strings,

dalliance with the meanings of things.

The slow sound of awakening

stirs us at morning light

to remind that life is never-ending.

We love

we live

we dance

we sleep unknowing.

My soul aches and sighs,

wakes and cries

a long slow moan

that lasts until dawn,

drives me

and calls me to the dance.

Sullen sadness

sunken eyes

swimming in confusion.

Anticipation,

trepidation and sighs,

reality or illusion,

deception of delusion,

truth or lies.

The truth doesn't cut like a knife

    or broken glass

        but clean and slick

            like a paper cut

                bandaged with smiles

                    disguised in etiquette.

You write of all the emotions

    I hold in my heart.

You know my secrets,

    secrets you have been told before

        by other sailors.

Your eyes see so clearly

    and I am awed at the perception.

I dream of knowing you,

    yet cannot fathom the depths of your soul,

        your mysteries yet to unfold.

Do you hear my voice?

    Voce allegretto!

        Do you sense my being?

          Crescendo!

Do I invade your dreams?

    Is what happens what it seems

        or just illusion

            deception

                your deft slight of hand?

Yes, boys bring you azaleas,

    men buy you booze,

        woman bring the regalia,

            lovers give you what you choose.

You take what you need and leave the rest behind

    and no one has the nerve to call you unkind.

Faith

    a word I have searched for

        long and hard.

Faith in my soul,

    my spirit,

      my heart,

        but I still long for the white lines of the highway.

Ride and remember,

    ride and forget

      ride to a life

        you haven't lived yet.

LA, Chicago, New Orleans

    anywhere

      where no one cares

        who you have been

          or who you want to be.

FREEWHEELING

Racing down the road

    freewheeling,

        cycling into the future

            he rides.

Not worrying about where or when,

    consequence or remembrance,

        only feeling the wind in his face,

            stinging his cheeks,

                the blood in his veins.

His heart, pounding to the rhythm of his soul,

    swerving,

        sliding,

            gliding on the edge

                oblivious to the danger,

    alive with the thrill of speed,

    the power of control, he rolls,

        until with a grand triumphant loop,

            he reaches the end of his down hill ride.

Then with renewed spirit,

    washed with exhilaration,

        steeled with determination.

            he begins the ardous journey back up.

Stroke after painful stroke,

    he pushes the pedals,

        keeps the wheels turning at all cost,

            never lets his feet touch solid ground.

Never wavering

    his focus aimed on the summit,

        where with one deep breath,

        he can slowly turn,

gather his courage,

gaze into oblivion

    and begin another plunge into destiny.

Racing down the road

    freewheeling.

NUMBER NINE

I have never felt so alone

    as I do at this moment

        minute

           hour

                space in time.

The desire to fulfill the quest is fading.

There is no La Mancha for me to return to.

      El Dorado has tarnished in the setting sun

        and I can find no Sancho

          to ride

              by my side

I lay crying to Mother Ocean

      tearing pages from the I Ching,

        cursing my heart.

The marrow of my bones

    dries

        brittle

           with the longing for peace,

          knowledge,

            truth,

              love.

I dream of easy times

    when the summer wind was my lover.

We would dance with our friends

    the trees,

        court the stars

            and sing our hearts' song.

But now my riddles,

    like ancient mariner's rhymes,

        fall on deaf ears.

Passers-by who drop a penny in my cup

    out of pity

        and social circumstance

            they care not

                to look

                    inside.

OUT OF BODY

As the blood runneth

    life permeates

        my being.

I am at once

    there and gone,

        lifted,

        buoyant,

looking back at my body,

    wondering why I see myself

        as death would have me.

        Still

my heart beats too loud.

I AM SO TIRED OF QUIET DESPERATION

You act as if my confidence was expected, not treasured.

I have given you all I have to give,

must you toss it aside as if it didn't exist?

I too live in darkness,

the black hole of longing from which I fear there may

be no escape.

Everyday is a new challenge.

Everyday the voices are louder,

the gun is closer

and I have to look in the mirror and say not today.

I understand your love.

I love too,

and my love is no less important.

Yes, your love is all consuming

you are aflame

I can feel the heat.

But that heat does little to warm my soul.

no need to apologize,

we play the cards we are dealt.

Just try to remember that behind all the facades

    the smiles,

        the jokes,

            the drunken momentary anesthesia,

  I am

    also

      a man.

BEULAH'S THREE AM

Another night,

    life's cycle goes around.

Another night,

    the clock clicks closer

        to the tolling of the bell.

Night after night

    night into day

        day into night

            the clock ticks away

                as life's longings lay

        unfulfilled.

Tick, tock

    the unstoppable clock

      swings it's hands and pulls you with them

        around the face of the time piece of life.

Another night

    into day.

VAMPIRES ON HOLD

The night bled

    and dripped on us.

We drank

    and found LeStat's phone number.

We called

    and waited for the wind to drive the rain

        enough

            to wash our souls.

Sated but unsatisfied,

    we searched

        for light in the mist,

            new blood.

The rain glistened across the passing plain,

    time transcended beyond and the present realm

        dissolved into past impressions

Our hearts throbbed

    and wondered where they were

        and we slowly became

            aware

that Humanity has no

    sense of reality.

A QUIET PLACE

I have to go now and sit in a quiet place,

    pick up the pieces of shattered dreams

        and illusions that surround me.

I need a psychic broom to sweep my soul clean,

    for I fear I will never be able to reassemble the wreckage

        the way it once was.

But then, why try?

I could just create a mosaic.

    a kaleidoscope of emotion to hide behind.

Spin the cycle and watch the ever changing patterns disguise my
      scars

    but in the eye of the beholder lies the danger of being unseen.

      The mirrors infinite image upon itself is still just one image.

It's hard to find a quiet place in the parade.

I can shut out the trumpets blare,

    the cymbals crash

        the passing crowds stare,

           but there's always that one lone piper

             playing O'Driscoll's song

It doesn't fade, but wafts over my soul

    and I am adrift in his "drear heart lake".

Is that the boatman of Styx I see?

    Sorry, I don't have a coin today.

I can sit in the somber cold of solitude.

    Sit and wait for Satori's slap

        but I have lost my Sensei.

I have left my fortress,

    bloodied my knuckles

        climbing the mountain to read the snow poets musings,

           only to find they have vanished,

             melted in longings warm windy breath.

I can only stare and wonder what might have been.

A quiet place,

    not dark,

        but filled with reality's stark light

           to shine through my kaleidoscope.

But I must not get lost in the shadow play,

    the shadows make you stray.

Is that,

    that damned piper again?

He and that horned fiddler play a merry tune,

        but I'll sit out the dance,

           in a quiet place.

CRUCIFIXION

Morning light shines over my pale soul

    illuminating my misery.

I wonder at the wavering wind.

Small birds peck my eyes

    as I lay like carrion,

        abandoned and dismissed by the passing
        hoard.

Too bound by my earthly fetters,

    I rail

        and curse those that have nailed me here.

I still believe in the promise,

    even as it lies broken before me.

Where are those easy days

    when the sun shone through a rainbow?

        Why is the sky so gray and bleak?

I catch the scent of gardenias and your hair

    mingling with the fume of my dripping blood

        and I feel time washing over me.

The tide turns and ebbs.

I plead to my angels

    but they slap me and say enough,

        now is your time they whisper.

This thorny mantle pierces my skin,

    my body is so tired and heavy

        and I am afraid of the sepulcher.

But the warm sun on my face

    sooths my fears and eases the pain of longing.

        new light, another day, another chance to die.

SHE SWAYS SO SENSUOUSLY

Do you like trees, I said?

I have a thing for the Trees,

    they're the dinosaurs of the plant world.

She stared at me as if I had lost all touch with reality,

    which I had

        but not at that moment.

It happened on a warm summer night in 1968.

I was wrestling with a cardboard box in Touro Park.

    when the Trees first spoke to me.

Their words filled me with terror

    and ecstasy

        and life,

            the perception and loving of

                has never been quite the same.

I frolicked around the park that night

    to the chorus of their songs,

        until I found myself covered with a chocolate milkshake

            in the company of a somewhat distraught Earth Mother

                at the Nightowl Café.

I want to dance, she said

    I did too,

        but to a different fiddler.

My fiddler plays the wind and soars aloft,

    chased by Chagall's horse,

        dances with the little people at the Plow and Stars

            and is not afraid to pluck the heartstrings.

She sways so sensuously,

    and I hear the Trees,

        singing,

            rustling with my fiddlers wind.

And I dream of the lightness of love,

    floating above the green leaves

        swirling hand in hand with romance's tumultuous tornado.

I'm starting to feel the liquor, she says.

Will you be offended if I ask you to take me home?

    And I hear the Old Sycamore groan

    and whisper

        persevere.

Ok, I say, but no milkshakes on the way.

COULD I BE THERE

Where do you go when you dream?

Do you walk the craggy cliffs of Cornwall,

staring through the ocean mist for sailing ships

and as the sun sinks into the sea,

scamper across gaping chasms on Dragon's Breath

to the solace of your citadel,

walk the parapet and listen for the clomp of chargers' hooves

and the clang of armor to signal your hero's return from his crusade?

Could I be sir Knight?

Or do you stroll the green glades of Sherwood,

flirting with Fauns and Fairies,

finding your way among the old Ent's forest,

following the rakish rogue to rob the rich,

revel in the soft clover of Nature's bower,

laugh, scheme, and thrill at your outlaw's side?

Could I steal your heart?

Perhaps you journey to nether worlds.

Running along the violet sand beach of an infrared ocean,

fleeing and fighting alien demon's who feed on the energy of your soul,

you stumble, tripping,

your laser jams,

and as the dark presence is about to consume you

the strong, sure hand of your vessel's commander

pulls you into his arms to safety.

Could I come to your rescue?

Maybe you find yourself dressed in white satin,

sitting at the roulette wheel,

gambling with love, life and intrigue,

trying to increase the gain for hidden secrets

enough to escape to a new life on a private island of sanity.

As the ball falls on red 7, the reluctant croupier slides you all
the chips

and the sinister, sallow-faced scoundrel

prepares to plunge a knife in your back

when the dagger's direction is discreetly redirected into the
heart of villainy

by the man in the white dinner jacket

who hands you a drink and your passport.

Could I be your Secret Agent?

Where do you go when you dream,

when slumber's soft touch pulls you from reality

in to the realm of magic, fantasy and inner truth?

And where you go,

Could I be there?

AS I KISS HER EYES

As I kiss her eyes,

I wonder if she can see the passion that has consumed my soul.

I can see the reflections of my life's wasted opportunities

    in the mirrors on the headboard.

The singe of single malt does little to quell the fears of life's longings.

I search for courage as she turns out the light.

Shudders of anticipation erupt across my flesh,

    as the warmth of her touch is emblazoned on my heart and mind.

I try to envelop her with rapacious embrace,

    pull her body into mine,

        capture her essence for all time

           and through some magical spiritual

osmosis

    unite our beings.

Her lips,

    sweet fruit of Eden's tree,

        beckon me on,

           lead me into the valley of my desire.

"You know just what you want, don't you?" she wryly asks

    her dark eyes staring through my translucent libido.

What I want?

I look up and stare into the headboard

    and in that moment of epiphany,

        all courage slips silently

           into the dark abyss of self doubt.

I sit like Henry on the eve of Agincourt,
cloaked against recognition,
        searching for the truth of being
                to prepare for battle.
Not ready to accept the possibility of defeat,
        my burning desire,
                the craving of my eternal longing,
                        the madness of my lust,
                                will not stay hidden.
I am compelled to shed my disguises,
mount my steed and ride into the valley to slay the dragon,
        but I am more Quixote than Saint George
                and this windmill has teeth.
Her hot moist breath
sweeps like Sirocco on the Sahara of my mind.
        I thirst for her,
                crawl to the oasis of her body,
                        to lap the sweet water of her well.
If I could just lay here
        in the warmth of her glow,
                sleep
                        in dark mystery
                                surrounded by the forest of her
hair.
Then, awaken to the burning light of each other's Promethean
flame,
        I could stand
                and hold her proudly
                        in the dawn of a new beginning.
Then suddenly,
        she softly reaches into my chest
                rips out my still bleeding heart
                        and says
"I'm going to have to ask you to go."

SESSION ON THE LEESIDE

As Erato's presence pervaded the room,
you shed your body's constraints
    and searched for the meaning of your soul.
Freed
    of worldly shackles,
        you danced,
            and felt the earth beneath your feet tremble.
Prowling
    for the feeling
        that releases long hidden emotions,
    you delved into the pit of your depths
        to regurgitate swallowed pride.
Reliving those moments once laid to rest
    you sang,
        your spirit exalting
            the songs of parted passions.

SPARKLES

The lights on the tree sparkled.
The conversation sparkled
Her eyes sparkled.
The snow sparkled.
The red and green shot glasses sparkled.
I sparkled like a firecracker whose fuse was lit
And could not be extinguished.
I was burning way too bright
Trying to recapture a flame that I hoped would attract my desire,
and although those flames of youth were now just glowing embers
They still burned so hot,
and I was throwing gasoline on the coals.
The explosion was sudden,
the dull thud of my face on the floor
and all the sparkles were lost in a sea of confusion and blackness.
I awoke
with that startled resurrection of reality,
as if night had not slipped into day
and time had been momentarily suspended.
I stared at the battered image in the mirror
and felt the shattered dreams in my chest,
like broken glass cutting, stabbing, shredding my heart.
I went to her,
lay beside her,
daring to hope that what I knew was true wasn't.
And in her voice, frigid enough to freeze boiling blood,

the one I had heard her use on an unenlightened shop clerk once,
she asked for her space back.
Words that rang like carbon steel,
pierced my heart as deep as any dagger
and shrouded my world in the pale of lost romance.
Silence consumed the atmosphere,
and as my eyes opened
all the sparkles vanished.

LEAP OF FAITH

I filled my mouth with sweet whiskey,
to wash away the bitter taste of jealousy.
> I bit my lip,
>> as my trembling hands, could not help but
>>> write the words.
I took them to her door
> and could not leave them,
>> left and came back,
tried to turn and walk away
> stood entranced,
>> staring into the future
until at last, I made that leap of faith
> across a chasm of no return.
I left the words for here eyes
> and though I may have leapt to the death of my passion
>> I had to save the soul of my being
>>> and let her hear the beating
>>>> of my true heart.
I filled my mouth once again with bourbon's bouquet
to dull the sense of doubt and longing
> that is my heart's requiem,
>> until I collapsed into the arms of Morpheus
>>> and could leap no more.

ODYSSEY

I watch a slow moon rise in a purple sky,

    and my heart wonders why

        her perfume suddenly fills my nostrils.

I remember her eyes,

    as I gaze at the shining orb

        balanced precariously

            between reality and fantasy.

Before me stretches a vast plane,

    Matisse's shadow trees line the edge of existence

        and shelter me from twilight's last meanderings.

Destiny and guardian angels

    fight for my wayward soul.

I hear the Sirens singing seductive syllables,

    luring me to craggy shores.

        I bite my lip,

        make fast my keel,

I delve and pitch in the oceans of illusion,

    shudder as the frigid waves break across my bow

On the shore,

    women in Italian leather

        wonder and stare,

            but are afraid to take a chance at rescue.

PSALM OF PERSEPHONE

Oh, my sweet Persephone,

    Princess trapped between two worlds

I lay beside you and bask in your Promethean flame

      try to kiss away the salty tears of consequence.

        I hear your heart pounding,

            a wild fawn fleeing the tiger close at
    hand,

     and nestle in your bosom to let you know you are not at bay.

I sing the hymns of new awakenings.

    songs of joy and happiness to be,

       to open the door of love.

And you spread your wings

    open your heart

      and take me inside,

         our eyes locked together

You hold me in the eternal grasp of the universe

    until I surrender and collapse

      in the warmth of your sanctity.

   Oh, my sweet Persephone.

WHEAT FIELD

I see the small cedars bending against the wind
    and my mind races
        back to my childhood,
where I would lay, starring at the clouds
    lost in the tall brown grass
        in the field where I went to escape reality.
The sun was warm
    and I could hide from the wind huddled in my covey hole.
My dreams were new and uncluttered,
    my eyes did not bleed
        and I was unafraid.
The wind danced across the hay
    restless and unchained,
        pines swayed and called to me.
    My heart was virginal and unused then,
But now, now the breeze is tainted with the feted odor of shattered dreams
    and suddenly in my mind
I see Vincent standing at his easel,
    the dust rising from his pacing.
I smell the oil on the canvas and on the muzzle
I gaze across the wheat as the fetid breeze drives the crows
into the air
    and then I know
        I understand his leaving and his dreams unfulfilled,
    I know.

I stare into my field

    and feel the despair of his passion,

       his loneliness.

The smell of the wind turns my head and I hear the trees chanting

    and I know, now I know.

PERSEPHONE IN PINK GLASSES

The fates and my muse are drunk
and dancing naked
in the moonlight.
I swim in the wake of their revelry
and flounder
on the shores of destiny
wondering
where the tides of life will wash my body next.
Fortune's winds blow across my existence.
The cool breeze
chills
my soul.
I shiver at the prospect of new beginnings
and shudder at the chance
of reliving
old lives.
My fingers are bloody from clawing at reality's wall.
I lay entombed
by hesitance and doubt
I dream of Persephone
dancing with me,
sailing across new oceans
adrift in wonder

Oh, Persephone let me touch your soul
As you have held mine.
Escape the dark underworld
And bask in the warm embrace
Of love's light with me
Before I drown
In this deep ocean of ambivalence.

THE PRICE OF ART

Once again

I climb the tall stoned steps to the altar,

pick up the sacred blade

plunge

rip and tear

flesh that is so fleeting

reach deep into the cavity I have laid bare.

Pull out my heart and hold it

Reaching high in the air.

Blood runs down my arms

covering the ground on which I stand

Mother Earth soaks it in

and hidden creatures feed.

It beats aloft so that all may see

some may mock,

some turn in fear,

some laugh with disdain.

some dance in merriment,

some revel in the passion

some share the pain.

But my true heart beats and bleeds

until it is dry and still,

spent and used,

and the crowd in silence has lost its will.

I then quickly return it

To the shell it gives life and pause

turn to face the throng

smile

and as if nothing ever happened,

descend to take my place among

the faceless.

BIRTHDAY

Time streaks
        through the universe.
             We gasp
                  and giggle
as it passes
        naked
across the pathos of our destiny
        and
in our dream of time past
        we recall
             images of the encounter
and wonder how it got so
             hairy.

SIX WHISKEYS

Truth and desire
    dance in limbo
stares and anticipation fuel the fire
Every one is searching
    for lust
      for love
        for consolation
          for forgiveness
We all dance
    some with less
        inhibition
Purloined perception
    A heart stolen by sensuous sirocco
eyes dart and are quickly averted
laughter pervades
        the senses
and in a brief moment
    love seems
        all too real

SKY DANCERS

Starlings streak
      arabesque across the azure void.
      Soaring in silent syncopation they ballet
an icy sun glares
      their sleek ebony bodies
          blind the audience.
Patron's hearts rise in ovation
      Standing breathless as a red-tailed raptor
         and fearless hero pas-de-deux
Slowly then swiftly,
      swirl and sway
         in timeless embrace of life's passions
until the drama is played out,
      dancers exit
         and patrons wipe a tear waiting for an encore.

End of the Day

Will my sunset come
    in the languid summer evening,
        lush with green life
when the sun lingers on the lips of night
      to fade into the soft light of a full moon,
as my eyes grow heavy
      I can hear the laughter of Tatiana and her maidens
        as they dance through the forest.
          and I long to join them.

Or will my night fall
    like a hard freeze in the depths of winter
        lost in the dark of the moon
          still
    covered with frost
        alone
        in the darkness?

Perhaps the autumn wind will cover my sunset
    with a shower of leaves
        wrap me in a bed of crimson and gold
          swathed with nature's long tresses,
the hair of my ancient lovers,
      the trees
        will embalm me
          as I lay warm in their embrace
      for the long sleep.

But I long for the time of rebirth when
            the soul of Mother Earth
                            stirs
sirens sing my dirge
                and fresh rain
                            washes my dying passions
                                    from my mind

I will fertilize the new rising
                and become part of what has always been.
As my sun sinks
            below
                        the arc of the sphere,
I care not when
            but that it comes with good tidings
                    and peace
                        and a song of
                                remembrance.

PART TWO

LEGBA WALKS

LEGBA WALKS

Time is racing by my window,
      dancing a sombulent sensory samba.
The couch offers little to ease the discomfort
      of my twitching
           soul.
Trumpets blare
      echos of termination resound in my
           brain.
Angels have visited me twice
      in my dreams
the kiss of the last
      still lingers on my libido.
           Lips so soft,
                yet strong and willing.
But there, in the distance
      Legba walks
           along the foggy bank
                of my subconscious river.
Cross-current of black water
      the delta
           of my abyss.
           and I am unable to stop the rushing tide.

A VISIT FROM ST. LANOUETTE

The Christmas Eve at the piano in the hall of mirrors

is seared into my unconscious being.

The dance was in full swing

to the rhythm of love, of discovery, of adventure.

When what to my wondering eyes appeared,

The Artist,

bearing gifts of beauty and enlightenment

and the keys called and beckoned me

into another universe.

I slammed them again and again until I bled

I gave them my heart and soul

I sat listless

after the passion,

gazed at the reflections.

Where was I?

Did it matter?

Suddenly Sensei slaps me back to his reality

and then in a twinkling I heard from above

the screams of lovers and lost souls

adrift in the moonlit snow.

AZALEAS BY THE WINDOW

The cool breeze laced with the scent of Azalea
caresses my soul.
I am thankful for the senses to feel the embrace
and watch yellow butterflies dance on the pink petals.
The azure sky beckons my heart,
the trees sway in samba with the wind
as the rhythm of life pulsates through my being
and love is the dance

TIE - DYE NAP

I was trying to take a nap
    at a Hippie Festival
        when this couple started doing
a Fibber McGhee and Molly routine over the microphone
    that they didn't know was on.
I sighed, lifted my head and gazed
    bleary eyed
        out on the dusty landscape
the veldt was covered in Hippies
    everywhere
    like the great herds of bison from a bygone era
filling the basin
    wallowing in the sand
        tie-dyed bodies oozing with sweat
          snorting and roaring
            beneath the full moon.
So I slowly rose
    strapped on my weapon
        and Fibber, Molly and I played another set.
The Hippies danced into oblivion.

MIDNIGHT AT THE BARRE

As we dance to the rhythm of life
    I try to avoid stepping on her toes
        but it's her hands that fascinate me.
She catches me staring at them,
    sleek, artful, full of passion
        she caresses her glass as if it were a lover
        every movement a seduction of my soul.
I sigh and sip my wine
    knowing that I will never feel that touch;
        she will never even know my name.
Age creates a wall and few have the courage
    to climb the ladder
        but everyone
        wants to see
            the other side
                and samba in the greener grass.

LAST DANCE

Small birds peck at my eyes
as I lay in this barren landscape.
I cannot move.
Their beaks puncture my soul and I bleed,
life ebbs from my static body
and I am resolved for the end.
Trees in the distance bow with the dissolute wind.
I dream of our last dance
your body's sensuous soliloquy
enveloping my being
the warm touch of our bodies melding
the sudden pain of the knife in my ribs.
Was the truth worth my demise?
I defended my heart
and paid the consequence.
now I lay dying in this barren landscape
feeding my soul to the gathering flock
I cannot move
and I am resolved for the end.

PERSPECTIVE

The play of time and experience

    dances across my perspective,

        I wonder

and wish for new beginnings.

    The gap

        between lust and love grows wider

            and I lack the skill to bridge

    the chasm.

I still revel in the abandon

    and lust

        for the uninhibited life,

the dreams that died at Altamont

    I question

    I wonder

        I live for today

    and love being.

THE NIGHT BIRD

The night bird sings
    she flirts with her warble
and I am drawn to her presence,
    but she darts and scampers away
      still filling the air with her song,
        never coming close enough to touch.
The stars and the soft summer night are her orchestra
she performs her aria
    and bows to the applause of her flock
   safe and distant
    she warbles on

           into the still night air.

LEAVES IN THE WIND

The rustle of leaves in the wind

portends

the space

between reality and perception.

A misheard word

can lead to

love or disgust.

An unintentional touch

may be the beginning

or the end.

It depends,

on what you hear

as the leaves rustle in the wind

FLOUNDER

Erato has abandoned me

I lay on my back

a fish out of water

flapping my fins and tail

gasping for breath

staring destiny in the face

wondering

if I will ever find the stream where it all began
again

Alone is such a treacherous word

when in reality it is just ennui

I need a soul taser to restart my dreams

so I can once again live life in a waking state

but sleep is so enticing and demands nothing

Stand and deliver

the ancient outlaws demanded

I wish to do neither.

take the loot

I have no use for it now.

TIME FLOWS

Time Flows.

Racing past the gathering crowd of onlookers

currents, turbulent and unrelenting, wash over us.

We clutch at floating debris

and struggle against the rising tide,

but the raging river of time is flooding

out of control,

and we are doomed to drown in the depths of it.

Then suddenly, amidst the chaos and confusion

clarity,

a light at the end of the tunnel vision.

The vagaries of life fall away

into the abyss of unconscious bliss.

You order another drink and care not for

the outcome or circumstance.

TOURNIQUET

She grabbed my arm

    and told me I didn't know

        how time heals wounds

           so slow.

I stared at her

    and beyond her dark eyes I see her languid lips.

    She parts them

and opens the wounds of past conflicts,

    epic jousts of words and music

        in the forbidden realm of lost love.

The blood of passion

    rises and flows

        and I have no tourniquet.

WANING MOON

The waning moon

    makes my head throb and my heart ache

        like a bad hangover or crashing from a bad trip,

It sits in the dark night sky laughing and whispering

        "what could have been."

The waning moon

    still shines

        but just portends the darkness to come

        It's light ebbing from my soul and making me

            regret the eventide.

The waning moon

    drains my being

        and erases the sparkle of the stars in my heart

            replacing it with loneliness and dread.

The waning moon

    displaces the magic of life

        with the monotony of existence

            and steals the joy of lunacy.

Damn you waning moon!

DELIRIUM

The light of a burning moon
glints from the scimitar delicately balanced on her pate
her hands weave exotic tales of ecstasy and fate.
Soft supple limbs glide in sublime motion
hips sway with the tides of oceans.
But it's her eyes,
clear, bright, staring into your soul
mesmerizing your heart to her control.
Holding you rapt unable to look away,
you are snared by the embrace and cannot stray.
Imprisoned by her,
caged in the trance,
she holds your heart in the desire of the dance.

MIMOSA

Mimosa memories
        waft across the landscape of my childhood.
            It was my Mother's tree.
I watch the delicate puffs of pink floss
                dance in the sultry summer breeze
        and I can feel her with me
guiding me along the path of my being
        telling me
        to let the sanguine sunset linger in my heart
            and embrace the mimosa's
                magic
                    mystery.

EPITAPH

I crawl across the mountain glade covered with snow

pick up a fallen branch to write my epitaph,

but my hands are too frozen to inscribe my thoughts.

The sun glistens through

     bending branches

     of trees above me

and I wonder if my life will melt

     before my quest is fulfilled.

I stop,

     stand,

     gaze at the moment

     and it is done.

CPSIA information can be obtained
at www.ICGtesting.com
Printed in the USA
FFOW01n2004090617
36482FF

9 781942 081111